**WHAT
GOOD
SHALL
I DO
THIS
DAY?**

WHAT GOOD SHALL I DO THIS DAY?

A JOURNAL INSPIRED BY

BENJAMIN FRANKLIN

CHRONICLE BOOKS

SAN FRANCISCO

ISBN: 978-1-4521-6846-3

Manufactured in China.

Designed by Kristen Hewitt

10 9 8 7 6 5 4 3 2 1

Chronicle books and gifts are available at special
quantity discounts to corporations, professional
associations, literacy programs, and other orga-
nizations. For details and discount information,
please contact our premiums department at
corporatesales@chroniclebooks.com or at
1-800-759-0190.

Chronicle Books LLC
680 Second Street
San Francisco, California 94107
www.chroniclebooks.com

WHAT GOOD SHALL I DO THIS DAY?

HOW TO USE THIS JOURNAL

Starting from two simple daily questions, this journal helps you think about your life the way Benjamin Franklin thought about his. Franklin was introspective, curious, lighthearted, and forever on the lookout for a quicker path from Point A to Point B. Were he alive today, there is no doubt he would be a wildly popular self-improvement guru, topping bestseller lists and selling out convention centers while touting his helpful maxims and utilitarian approach to life's many problems.

But what would set Franklin apart from modern day self-help aficionados is what he saw as the underlying purpose of changing your life for the better. For Franklin, becoming a better person wasn't about peacocking your perfection over others, or even achieving financial or social success; its primary purpose was to make a person of better use to her or his community. Simply put, it was about doing good works.

As Franklin rightly saw it, the more you work toward doing good, the more you improve your own life, which helps you do more good, which helps you improve your own life. As the days pass by, this approach becomes a kind of personal perpetual-motion machine in which each step forward gives you the fuel to meet your next challenge.

Many of the following pages feature Franklin's two daily prompts, which he asked himself in his own journal:

What good shall I do this day?

What good have I done this day?

Use these pages as a thoughtful record of your goals and aspirations for the day to come. Be honest with yourself and try to not overreach—chart out your overarching goals, but think of the small things you can do each day that will help you work toward larger accomplishments. Your daily good can be something as simple as spending five minutes with an elderly neighbor, taking a moment to research a worthy cause, or even choosing to avoid an indulgent expense at the grocery store. It can be more grandiose, but remember that Franklin defined goodness through utility. Think about ways, on a daily basis, you can be actively useful to yourself, your family, your community, your country, and the world.

At the end of each day, spend a few moments to review your progress, both your advances and your setbacks. What are you curious about that you might not have been at the start of the day? What are the challenges you faced? What ways can you do better tomorrow?

On other pages, you will find specific writing prompts that are inspired by the deep well of Franklin's writings and philosophies. Think of these as off-the-cuff homework assignments, to be considered and completed on a timeline of your choosing. You may find they relate directly to a challenge or idea you're already engaged in, or they may propel you to consider something entirely new. Sprinkled throughout these pages you will also find quotes from Franklin to surprise, amuse, and inspire you.

The crux of this journal, as was the crux of Franklin's own journey toward what he called "moral perfection," is simplicity. Don't fret too hard at the setbacks you face or about the slow pace you might make toward your own personal goalposts. Remember, too, that part of Franklin's success hinged on not taking himself or his goals too seriously. Of his failure to obtain the perfection he wished for himself, he joked that "a benevolent man should allow a few Faults in himself, to keep his Friends in Countenance."

BENJAMIN FRANKLIN AND THE PRACTICAL APPROACH TO PERFECTION

A BRIEF HISTORICAL SKETCH

"It was about this time that I conceiv'd the bold and arduous Project of arriving at Moral Perfection," wrote Benjamin Franklin in 1784, an old man looking back at his younger self with what we can imagine was a hint of a smile. Moral perfection? Surely a man of reason like Franklin knew the impossibility of such a task?

The fact was, however, that despite being one of the most sublime and versatile of the Enlightenment thinkers, an exacting scientist, a canny inventor, and a consummate businessman, as well one of the preeminent pioneers of American democracy, Benjamin Franklin was not a conventionally "reasonable" man. By reasonable in this instance we mean moderate, tame, tamped down by protocol and decorum. Franklin was untamable except when he found utility in being tamed, such as when in order to secure credit for his printing business he "took care to not only be in reality industrious and frugal, but to avoid all appearances to the contrary." Let us consider just a few hallmarks from his life and times: He was a man who ran away from home at the age of seventeen, illegally fleeing a term of indentured service to his older brother. He was a partner in a common-law marriage and the father of an illegitimate child at a time when such things were considered black marks on one's character. He was a lifelong incorrigible flirt, continually engaged in a series of romantic dalliances that sparked gossip and outrage but that always fell just shy of adultery. He retired from his profitable printing business at the age of forty-three to better pursue his scientific curiosity and spend more time doing good works. He was known to hide a vial of oil in a secret compartment in the tip of his cane so he could secretly drop it into ponds and streams and thus amaze his friends with his "magic" power to calm turbulent waters. At seventy, suffering from gout and kidney stones, Franklin embarked on a dangerous winter trip into the Canadian wilderness to meet with besieged American forces during the dawn of the Revolutionary War. And a few years later, at an age when most men of the time were confined to their beds (if not indeed their graves), he crossed the Atlantic and spent years in the courts of Versailles, arranging and managing France's assistance in the war effort, surrounded by hostile spies and cooed over by glamorous women.

Benjamin Franklin might have been unreasonable, but he was practical. As his biographer Walter Isaacson noted, Franklin "based his creed on rational utility." To be of use was of primary importance to Franklin. His scientific pursuits were all the more exciting to him when they revealed a useful application, such as his famous discovery of the electrical properties of lightning, which led from his fanciful kite and key to the invention and widespread use of lightning rods. Even his magic trick with the oil in his cane arose from his desire to determine whether or not oil could be used to "moderate the Violence of the Waves" and ease the passage of ships through dangerous waters.

Franklin's social endeavors were also gilded with practical outcomes. At the age of twenty-one, he founded a club of his peers in Philadelphia, the Junto, whose purpose was to foster moral improvements of its members and civic improvements at large. That a happy—and not unlooked for—side effect of the Junto was that Franklin soon found the group's members "exerting themselves in recommending business" to his fledgling printing shop does not diminish its relevance. As always with Franklin, personal growth grew out of civic duty. Proposals from the Junto led to the founding of America's first subscription library, now the oldest continually operating public institution in the United States, and to a variety of social proposals for the colonies, including establishing volunteer fire brigades and night-watch police forces paid for by local taxes. Franklin's good works spread from the Junto outward. He founded the University of Pennsylvania in 1751, and until he was fired by the British in 1774, he was one of the two joint deputy postmasters of the colonies, reforming the colonial postal service to make it both more efficient and profitable as well as personally surveying more than 1,600 miles of postal routes. The Continental Congress reappointed Franklin as the first postmaster general in 1775.

To such a man, especially the young and impetuous and gracefully witty man Franklin was in early adulthood, a plan for achieving "moral perfection" would not have seemed impractical. Arduous and bold? Yes, but not impractical. The operative word here of course is "plan." Developing a plan toward moral perfection is different than living a life of moral perfection. Franklin saw much benefit in concentrating on the process and worrying less about the outcome of his task. "I never arrived at the Perfection I had been so ambitious of obtaining," he wrote in his autobiography, "yet I was by the Endeavour made a better and happier Man than I otherwise would have been, if I had not attempted it."

Franklin began his plan by developing a list of thirteen virtues compiled from religious and philosophical readings and based on his own experience and judgment (you can read the list of Franklin's Thirteen Virtues and his accompanying explanations at the end of this journal). From temperance to silence, to frugality and humility, Franklin wanted to "acquire the Habitude" of these virtues, believing that the only way to do so was through the steady replacement of bad habits with good ones. To succeed, the task would require vigilance "against the unremitting Attraction of ancient Habits," and what better gatekeeper of orderly vigilance than a record book? That which can be recorded can be changed, and each little advancement grows upon the next. Keeping track of his daily accomplishments and setbacks allowed Franklin to create a logbook of personal improvement.

Opening his "little book" with a series of inspirational mottos, including quotations from Cicero and the Proverbs of Solomon, Franklin filled its pages with a simple check-box system to record both his victories and setbacks for each of the thirteen virtues. At the close of the day, Franklin would mark the page with "a little black Spot every Fault I found upon Examination to have been committed respecting that Virtue upon that Day." The goal was to reduce the occurrence of black spots day by day and week by week, focusing his attentions primarily on one virtue at a time for the duration of a week.

In the course of his study of the virtue of Order, Franklin developed a schedule for his ideal day, desiring that "every Part of my business should have its allotted Time." Franklin marked out a schedule for twenty-four hours, beginning with "Rise, wash, and address Powerful Goodness" and ending in the evening, after supper, music, or conversation, with an "examination of the day."

On the left margin of his daily schedule were two fill-in prompts, one at the top of the page, one at the bottom. The prompts speak for themselves:

The morning question, What good shall I do this day?	5	Rise, wash, and address *Powerful Goodness;* contrive day's business and take the resolution of the day; prosecute the present study; and breakfast.
	6	
	7	
	8	Work.
	9	
	10	
	11	
	12	Read or overlook my accounts, and dine.
	1	
	2	Work.
	3	
	4	
	5	
	6	Put things in their places, supper, music, or diversion, or conversation; examination of the day.
	7	
	8	
	9	
Evening question, What good have I done today?	10	
	11	
	12	
	1	Sleep.
	2	
	3	
	4	

Example of Benjamin Franklin's schedule of daily practices

The Morning Question, What Good shall I do this Day?

The Evening Question, What Good have I done this Day?

These simple questions are emblematic of Franklin's genius and his particular brand of practical self-improvement. It's simple, slightly whimsical, and requires no more than honesty and a keen sense of observation. What better way to approach each day, no matter what stress or challenge awaits you, than as a singular opportunity to do something good?

WHAT GOOD SHALL I DO THIS DAY?

_____

_____

_____

_____

_____

_____

_____

WHAT GOOD DID I DO THIS DAY?

_____

_____

_____

_____

_____

_____

_____

_____

Date

WHAT GOOD SHALL I DO THIS DAY?

_____

_____

_____

_____

_____

_____

_____

WHAT GOOD DID I DO THIS DAY?

_____

_____

_____

_____

_____

_____

_____

_____
Date

Think of someone in your own community, family, or workplace who deserves praise for a recent worthy action. What was the action? What do you admire about this person? In what way can you help them or help further the action they took?

_____

_____

_____

_____

_____

_____

_____

_____

_____

_____

_____

_____

_____

_____

_____

_____

_____

_____

_____

Date

WHAT GOOD SHALL I DO THIS DAY?	WHAT GOOD DID I DO THIS DAY?

Date

WHAT GOOD SHALL I DO THIS DAY?	WHAT GOOD DID I DO THIS DAY?

Date

Ignorance is often attended with Credulity when Knavery would mislead it, and with suspicion when honesty would set it right.

WHAT GOOD SHALL I DO THIS DAY?	WHAT GOOD DID I DO THIS DAY?

Date

WHAT GOOD SHALL I DO THIS DAY?

_____

_____

_____

_____

_____

_____

_____

WHAT GOOD DID I DO THIS DAY?

_____

_____

_____

_____

_____

_____

_____

_____
Date

WHAT GOOD SHALL I DO THIS DAY?	WHAT GOOD DID I DO THIS DAY?
_____	_____
_____	_____
_____	_____
_____	_____
_____	_____

_____
Date

WHAT GOOD SHALL I DO THIS DAY?	WHAT GOOD DID I DO THIS DAY?
_____	_____
_____	_____
_____	_____
_____	_____
_____	_____

_____
Date

What have you read lately—articles, novels, op-eds—that challenged you or aided you?

_____

_____

_____

_____

_____

_____

_____

_____

_____

_____

_____

_____

_____

_____

_____

_____

_____

_____

_____
Date

WHAT GOOD SHALL I DO THIS DAY?

_____

_____

_____

_____

_____

_____

_____

WHAT GOOD DID I DO THIS DAY?

_____

_____

_____

_____

_____

_____

_____

_____
Date

I am not insensible of the Impossibility of pleasing all,
but I would not willingly displease any.

WHAT GOOD SHALL I DO THIS DAY?	WHAT GOOD DID I DO THIS DAY?

Date

WHAT GOOD SHALL I DO THIS DAY?

_____

_____

_____

_____

_____

_____

_____

WHAT GOOD DID I DO THIS DAY?

_____

_____

_____

_____

_____

_____

_____

_____
Date

WHAT GOOD SHALL I DO THIS DAY?

_____

_____

_____

_____

_____

_____

_____

WHAT GOOD DID I DO THIS DAY?

_____

_____

_____

_____

_____

_____

_____

_____
Date

Think of a time in your life when planning and self-control helped you achieve a desired goal. Can you use this experience to help achieve a current goal?

_____

_____

_____

_____

_____

_____

_____

_____

_____

_____

_____

_____

_____

_____

_____

_____

_____
Date

He that has once done you a kindness will be more ready to do
you another, than he whom you yourself have obliged.

WHAT GOOD SHALL I DO THIS DAY?	WHAT GOOD DID I DO THIS DAY?

Date

WHAT GOOD SHALL I DO THIS DAY?	WHAT GOOD DID I DO THIS DAY?

Date

WHAT GOOD SHALL I DO THIS DAY?	WHAT GOOD DID I DO THIS DAY?

Date

List five people you turn to or would like to turn to for advice. Is there a current matter any of these people can help you with?

_____

_____

_____

_____

_____

_____

_____

_____

_____

_____

_____

_____

_____

_____

_____

_____

_____

Date

To pour forth benefits for the common good is divine.

WHAT GOOD SHALL I DO THIS DAY?	WHAT GOOD DID I DO THIS DAY?

Date

WHAT GOOD SHALL I DO THIS DAY?

_____

_____

_____

_____

_____

_____

_____

WHAT GOOD DID I DO THIS DAY?

_____

_____

_____

_____

_____

_____

_____

_____
Date

In what way can you be of service to humankind, your country, or a friend? What simple actions can you take that might address a specific issue, even if only in a small way?

_____

_____

_____

_____

_____

_____

_____

_____

_____

_____

_____

_____

_____

_____

_____

_____

Date

If you would keep your secret from an enemy,
tell it not to a friend.

WHAT GOOD SHALL I DO THIS DAY?	WHAT GOOD DID I DO THIS DAY?

Date

WHAT GOOD SHALL I DO THIS DAY?

_____

_____

_____

_____

_____

_____

_____

WHAT GOOD DID I DO THIS DAY?

_____

_____

_____

_____

_____

_____

_____

_____

Date

WHAT GOOD SHALL I DO THIS DAY?

WHAT GOOD DID I DO THIS DAY?

Date

Success can often be emulated through action. Who in your community or workplace is thriving? To what do you attribute their success?

_____

_____

_____

_____

_____

_____

_____

_____

_____

_____

_____

_____

_____

_____

_____

_____

_____
Date

WHAT GOOD SHALL I DO THIS DAY?	WHAT GOOD DID I DO THIS DAY?

Date

WHAT GOOD SHALL I DO THIS DAY?	WHAT GOOD DID I DO THIS DAY?

Date

I would rather have it said he lived usefully, than died rich.

WHAT GOOD SHALL I DO THIS DAY?	WHAT GOOD DID I DO THIS DAY?

Date

WHAT GOOD SHALL I DO THIS DAY?

_____

_____

_____

_____

_____

_____

_____

WHAT GOOD DID I DO THIS DAY?

_____

_____

_____

_____

_____

_____

_____

_____

Date

WHAT GOOD SHALL I DO THIS DAY?	WHAT GOOD DID I DO THIS DAY?

Date

WHAT GOOD SHALL I DO THIS DAY?	WHAT GOOD DID I DO THIS DAY?

Date

What is a common mistake or misstep you witness other people make? How can you avoid making this mistake yourself?

_____

_____

_____

_____

_____

_____

_____

_____

_____

_____

_____

_____

_____

_____

_____

_____

_____

_____

_____

_____

Date

WHAT GOOD SHALL I DO THIS DAY?

WHAT GOOD DID I DO THIS DAY?

Date

42

What good Men may do separately is small compared
with what they may do collectively.

WHAT GOOD SHALL I DO THIS DAY?	WHAT GOOD DID I DO THIS DAY?

Date

WHAT GOOD SHALL I DO THIS DAY?

WHAT GOOD DID I DO THIS DAY?

Date

WHAT GOOD SHALL I DO THIS DAY?

WHAT GOOD DID I DO THIS DAY?

Date

Especially on a local or community level, are there any laws or policies that you feel are ill-conceived or dangerous? Whether it's writing a letter to a representative or attending a community meeting, consider what you might do to help the situation.

_____

_____

_____

_____

_____

_____

_____

_____

_____

_____

_____

_____

_____

_____

_____

_____

_____

_____

_____
Date

Knowledge is obtained by the use of the ear
rather than the tongue.

WHAT GOOD SHALL I DO THIS DAY?	WHAT GOOD DID I DO THIS DAY?

Date

WHAT GOOD SHALL I DO THIS DAY?	WHAT GOOD DID I DO THIS DAY?

Date

WHAT GOOD SHALL I DO THIS DAY?	WHAT GOOD DID I DO THIS DAY?

Date

Write about someone new to your life—a coworker, a friend, an adversary. What do you admire about them? How can you be of help to them?

_____

_____

_____

_____

_____

_____

_____

_____

_____

_____

_____

_____

_____

_____

_____

_____

_____

_____

_____

Date

He that spits against the wind, spits in his own face.

WHAT GOOD SHALL I DO THIS DAY?	WHAT GOOD DID I DO THIS DAY?

Date

WHAT GOOD SHALL I DO THIS DAY?

_____

_____

_____

_____

_____

_____

_____

WHAT GOOD DID I DO THIS DAY?

_____

_____

_____

_____

_____

_____

_____

_____
Date

Have you been wronged recently? Was it a trifle or something serious? Think of positive ways you might resolve the situation and people you can reach out to for assistance.

_____

_____

_____

_____

_____

_____

_____

_____

_____

_____

_____

_____

_____

_____

_____

_____

_____

_____

_____

Date

The world is too full of Compliments already, they choke
the good plants of Benevolence and Beneficence.

WHAT GOOD SHALL I DO THIS DAY?	WHAT GOOD DID I DO THIS DAY?

Date

WHAT GOOD SHALL I DO THIS DAY?

WHAT GOOD DID I DO THIS DAY?

Date

WHAT GOOD SHALL I DO THIS DAY?

_____

_____

_____

_____

_____

_____

_____

WHAT GOOD DID I DO THIS DAY?

_____

_____

_____

_____

_____

_____

_____

_____
Date

List three people whom you feel it would be beneficial for you to know better—they can be from anywhere, work, your community, even your family. How do you propose to learn more about them?

_____

_____

_____

_____

_____

_____

_____

_____

_____

_____

_____

_____

_____

_____

_____

_____

_____

_____

_____
Date

WHAT GOOD SHALL I DO THIS DAY?	WHAT GOOD DID I DO THIS DAY?

Date

WHAT GOOD SHALL I DO THIS DAY?	WHAT GOOD DID I DO THIS DAY?

Date

Human felicity is produced by little advantages that occur every day.

WHAT GOOD SHALL I DO THIS DAY?	WHAT GOOD DID I DO THIS DAY?

Date

WHAT GOOD SHALL I DO THIS DAY?

WHAT GOOD DID I DO THIS DAY?

Date

WHAT GOOD SHALL I DO THIS DAY?	WHAT GOOD DID I DO THIS DAY?

Date

WHAT GOOD SHALL I DO THIS DAY?	WHAT GOOD DID I DO THIS DAY?

Date

"Lose no time. Be always employed in something useful." Where do you lose time in your day? Social media? Television? For a single day, try to abstain from something that is your biggest time-waster. Write about your results here.

_____

_____

_____

_____

_____

_____

_____

_____

_____

_____

_____

_____

_____

_____

_____

_____

_____

_____

_____

_____
Date

WHAT GOOD SHALL I DO THIS DAY?

WHAT GOOD DID I DO THIS DAY?

Date

We every day find men contending warmly on some point in Politicks, which, A'tho it may nearly concern them both, neither of them understand anymore than they do each other.

WHAT GOOD SHALL I DO THIS DAY?	WHAT GOOD DID I DO THIS DAY?

Date

WHAT GOOD SHALL I DO THIS DAY?

_____

_____

_____

_____

_____

_____

_____

WHAT GOOD DID I DO THIS DAY?

_____

_____

_____

_____

_____

_____

_____

_____
Date

WHAT GOOD SHALL I DO THIS DAY?

WHAT GOOD DID I DO THIS DAY?

Date

Both in the maxims of his *Poor Richard's Almanack* and in his study
of famous philosophers, Franklin was the master of the pithy, inspirational quotation. Find a quotation that speaks to you today and
write it here.

_____

_____

_____

_____

_____

_____

_____

_____

_____

_____

_____

_____

_____

_____

_____

_____

_____

_____
Date

Simplicity is the Homespun Dress of Honesty.

WHAT GOOD SHALL I DO THIS DAY?	WHAT GOOD DID I DO THIS DAY?

Date

WHAT GOOD SHALL I DO THIS DAY?	WHAT GOOD DID I DO THIS DAY?

Date

WHAT GOOD SHALL I DO THIS DAY?	WHAT GOOD DID I DO THIS DAY?

Date

"Put things in their places." Spend a few moments considering where in your life you are most disorganized. Is it physical disorganization or clutter, or is it more of a mental state? Write a to-do list of five simple steps you can take to better organize your life.

_____

_____

_____

_____

_____

_____

_____

_____

_____

_____

_____

_____

_____

_____

_____

_____

_____

_____
Date

WHAT GOOD SHALL I DO THIS DAY?

_____

_____

_____

_____

_____

_____

_____

WHAT GOOD DID I DO THIS DAY?

_____

_____

_____

_____

_____

_____

_____

_____
Date

WHAT GOOD SHALL I DO THIS DAY?

_____

_____

_____

_____

_____

_____

_____

WHAT GOOD DID I DO THIS DAY?

_____

_____

_____

_____

_____

_____

_____

_____

Date

Who was ever cunning enough to conceal his being so?
No Mask ever hid itself.

WHAT GOOD SHALL I DO THIS DAY?	WHAT GOOD DID I DO THIS DAY?

Date

WHAT GOOD SHALL I DO THIS DAY?

_____

_____

_____

_____

_____

_____

_____

WHAT GOOD DID I DO THIS DAY?

_____

_____

_____

_____

_____

_____

_____

_____
Date

WHAT GOOD SHALL I DO THIS DAY?

WHAT GOOD DID I DO THIS DAY?

Date

WHAT GOOD SHALL I DO THIS DAY?

WHAT GOOD DID I DO THIS DAY?

Date

Today's devotional: Franklin, quoting the Bible, believed in praising that which is "true, honest, just, pure, lovely, or of good report." Write a few sentences of praise or gratitude for something good in your life or the world at large.

_____

_____

_____

_____

_____

_____

_____

_____

_____

_____

_____

_____

_____

_____

_____

_____

_____

_____

_____

_____

Date

WHAT GOOD SHALL I DO THIS DAY?	WHAT GOOD DID I DO THIS DAY?

Date

WHAT GOOD SHALL I DO THIS DAY?	WHAT GOOD DID I DO THIS DAY?

Date

Most people dislike Vanity in others, whatever share
of it they have themselves.

WHAT GOOD SHALL I DO THIS DAY?	WHAT GOOD DID I DO THIS DAY?

Date

WHAT GOOD SHALL I DO THIS DAY?

_____

_____

_____

_____

_____

_____

_____

WHAT GOOD DID I DO THIS DAY?

_____

_____

_____

_____

_____

_____

_____

_____

Date

WHAT GOOD SHALL I DO THIS DAY?	WHAT GOOD DID I DO THIS DAY?

Date

WHAT GOOD SHALL I DO THIS DAY?	WHAT GOOD DID I DO THIS DAY?

Date

Make a list of five realistic ways you can be more charitable in your day-to-day life.

_____

_____

_____

_____

_____

_____

_____

_____

_____

_____

_____

_____

_____

_____

_____

_____

_____

_____

_____

_____

_____

_____

_____

_____

Date

WHAT GOOD SHALL I DO THIS DAY?

WHAT GOOD DID I DO THIS DAY?

Date

Self-denial is neither good nor bad, but as 'tis apply'd:
He that denies a Vicious Inclination is Virtuous
in proportion to his Resolution.

WHAT GOOD SHALL I DO THIS DAY?	WHAT GOOD DID I DO THIS DAY?

Date

WHAT GOOD SHALL I DO THIS DAY?

WHAT GOOD DID I DO THIS DAY?

Date

84

WHAT GOOD SHALL I DO THIS DAY?

_____

_____

_____

_____

_____

_____

_____

WHAT GOOD DID I DO THIS DAY?

_____

_____

_____

_____

_____

_____

_____

_____

Date

Use today's space to draft a letter of thanks or gratitude to an elected representative or community leader who you feel is doing good and important work.

_____

_____

_____

_____

_____

_____

_____

_____

_____

_____

_____

_____

_____

_____

_____

_____

Date

If we meet with crosses and disappointments, they are but as sour sauce to the sweet meats we enjoy, and the one hath not a right relish without the other.

WHAT GOOD SHALL I DO THIS DAY?	WHAT GOOD DID I DO THIS DAY?

Date

WHAT GOOD SHALL I DO THIS DAY?	WHAT GOOD DID I DO THIS DAY?

_____
Date

WHAT GOOD SHALL I DO THIS DAY?	WHAT GOOD DID I DO THIS DAY?

_____
Date

When was the last time you told someone an uncomfortable truth?

_____

_____

_____

_____

_____

_____

_____

_____

_____

_____

_____

_____

_____

_____

_____

_____

_____

_____

_____
Date

None but Fools are Knaves, for wise Men cannot help but be honest.

WHAT GOOD SHALL I DO THIS DAY?	WHAT GOOD DID I DO THIS DAY?

_____

Date

WHAT GOOD SHALL I DO THIS DAY?

_____

_____

_____

_____

_____

_____

_____

WHAT GOOD DID I DO THIS DAY?

_____

_____

_____

_____

_____

_____

_____

Date

If there was one aspect of your daily routine you could change, what would it be, and how might you change it?

_____

_____

_____

_____

_____

_____

_____

_____

_____

_____

_____

_____

_____

_____

_____

_____

_____

_____

_____

_____
Date

We protest and complain against the Falsehood and Treachery of Mankind, tho' the Remedy be always in our own Power, and each is at Liberty to reform himself.

WHAT GOOD SHALL I DO THIS DAY?	WHAT GOOD DID I DO THIS DAY?

Date

WHAT GOOD SHALL I DO THIS DAY?

_____

_____

_____

_____

_____

_____

_____

WHAT GOOD DID I DO THIS DAY?

_____

_____

_____

_____

_____

_____

_____

_____

Date

WHAT GOOD SHALL I DO THIS DAY?

WHAT GOOD DID I DO THIS DAY?

Date

Do you have any goals in your life that you are embarrassed to share because they too lofty or grandiose? Write one of them here, and spend some time thinking about a small step you can take toward that goal.

_____

_____

_____

_____

_____

_____

_____

_____

_____

_____

_____

_____

_____

_____

_____

_____

_____

_____
Date

WHAT GOOD SHALL I DO THIS DAY?	WHAT GOOD DID I DO THIS DAY?
_____	_____
_____	_____
_____	_____
_____	_____
_____	_____

Date

WHAT GOOD SHALL I DO THIS DAY?	WHAT GOOD DID I DO THIS DAY?
_____	_____
_____	_____
_____	_____
_____	_____
_____	_____

Date

Trust not a single person with the government of your state.

WHAT GOOD SHALL I DO THIS DAY?	WHAT GOOD DID I DO THIS DAY?

Date

WHAT GOOD SHALL I DO THIS DAY?

_____

_____

_____

_____

_____

_____

_____

WHAT GOOD DID I DO THIS DAY?

_____

_____

_____

_____

_____

_____

_____

_____

Date

WHAT GOOD SHALL I DO THIS DAY?	WHAT GOOD DID I DO THIS DAY?

_____
Date

WHAT GOOD SHALL I DO THIS DAY?	WHAT GOOD DID I DO THIS DAY?

_____
Date

When was the last time you had to deal with the fallout of a mistake you made?

_____

_____

_____

_____

_____

_____

_____

_____

_____

_____

_____

_____

_____

_____

_____

_____

_____

_____

_____

Date

WHAT GOOD SHALL I DO THIS DAY?

_____

_____

_____

_____

_____

_____

_____

WHAT GOOD DID I DO THIS DAY?

_____

_____

_____

_____

_____

_____

_____

_____

Date

We learn by Chess the habit of not being discouraged by present appearance in the state of our affairs, and that of persevering in the search of resources.

WHAT GOOD SHALL I DO THIS DAY?	WHAT GOOD DID I DO THIS DAY?

Date

WHAT GOOD SHALL I DO THIS DAY?

_____

_____

_____

_____

_____

_____

_____

WHAT GOOD DID I DO THIS DAY?

_____

_____

_____

_____

_____

_____

_____

_____
Date

WHAT GOOD SHALL I DO THIS DAY?

_____

_____

_____

_____

_____

_____

_____

WHAT GOOD DID I DO THIS DAY?

_____

_____

_____

_____

_____

_____

_____

_____

Date

Research a scientific principle or phenomenon you are curious about, and write a simple explanation of it here, in no more than five sentences. A few ideas: Do you know how a microchip works? What causes static electricity? Where does morning dew come from?

_____

_____

_____

_____

_____

_____

_____

_____

_____

_____

_____

_____

_____

_____

_____

_____

Date

'Tis a pity that Good Works among some sorts of People are so little Valued, and Good Words admired in their Stead.

WHAT GOOD SHALL I DO THIS DAY?	WHAT GOOD DID I DO THIS DAY?

_____
Date

WHAT GOOD SHALL I DO THIS DAY?	WHAT GOOD DID I DO THIS DAY?

Date

WHAT GOOD SHALL I DO THIS DAY?	WHAT GOOD DID I DO THIS DAY?

Date

What is the biggest frustration in your life right now? How would your life change if this frustration were resolved or removed?

_____

_____

_____

_____

_____

_____

_____

_____

_____

_____

_____

_____

_____

_____

_____

_____

_____

_____

_____

_____

Date

I imagine Hope and Faith may be more firmly built on Charity,
than Charity upon Faith and Hope.

WHAT GOOD SHALL I DO THIS DAY?	WHAT GOOD DID I DO THIS DAY?

_____
Date

WHAT GOOD SHALL I DO THIS DAY?

_____

_____

_____

_____

_____

_____

_____

WHAT GOOD DID I DO THIS DAY?

_____

_____

_____

_____

_____

_____

_____

_____
Date

List three places you'd like to travel to in the next year that would bring you joy and edification. These don't have to be exotic locales; they can be museums, parks, friends' home . . .

_____

_____

_____

_____

_____

_____

_____

_____

_____

_____

_____

_____

_____

_____

_____

_____

_____

_____
Date

Religion has often suffer'd when Orthodoxy is more regarded than Virtue.

WHAT GOOD SHALL I DO THIS DAY?	WHAT GOOD DID I DO THIS DAY?

Date

WHAT GOOD SHALL I DO THIS DAY?

_____

_____

_____

_____

_____

_____

_____

WHAT GOOD DID I DO THIS DAY?

_____

_____

_____

_____

_____

_____

_____

_____

Date

WHAT GOOD SHALL I DO THIS DAY?

_____

_____

_____

_____

_____

_____

_____

WHAT GOOD DID I DO THIS DAY?

_____

_____

_____

_____

_____

_____

_____

_____
Date

FRANKLIN'S VIRTUES:

• TEMPERANCE •

Eat not to dullness. Drink not to elevation.

===

Is there anything in your eating or drinking habits you would like to change? How would it help your life to do so? Would it improve your health? Your concentration? Etc.

_____

_____

_____

_____

_____

_____

_____

_____

_____

_____

_____

_____

_____

_____

_____

_____
Date

WHAT GOOD SHALL I DO THIS DAY?	WHAT GOOD DID I DO THIS DAY?

Date

WHAT GOOD SHALL I DO THIS DAY?	WHAT GOOD DID I DO THIS DAY?

Date

Write with the learned, pronounce with vulgar.

WHAT GOOD SHALL I DO THIS DAY?	WHAT GOOD DID I DO THIS DAY?

Date

WHAT GOOD SHALL I DO THIS DAY?

_____

_____

_____

_____

_____

_____

_____

WHAT GOOD DID I DO THIS DAY?

_____

_____

_____

_____

_____

_____

_____

_____

Date

WHAT GOOD SHALL I DO THIS DAY?	WHAT GOOD DID I DO THIS DAY?

Date

WHAT GOOD SHALL I DO THIS DAY?	WHAT GOOD DID I DO THIS DAY?

Date

· SILENCE ·

"Speak not but what may benefit others and yourself.
Avoid trifling conversation."

In what ways can you limit "trifling conversation" (either online or in person)?

_____

_____

_____

_____

_____

_____

_____

_____

_____

_____

_____

_____

_____

_____

Date

WHAT GOOD SHALL I DO THIS DAY?

WHAT GOOD DID I DO THIS DAY?

Date

The Noblest question in the world is What Good may I do in it?

WHAT GOOD SHALL I DO THIS DAY?	WHAT GOOD DID I DO THIS DAY?

Date

WHAT GOOD SHALL I DO THIS DAY?

_____

_____

_____

_____

_____

_____

_____

WHAT GOOD DID I DO THIS DAY?

_____

_____

_____

_____

_____

_____

_____

_____
Date

WHAT GOOD SHALL I DO THIS DAY?

_____

_____

_____

_____

_____

_____

_____

WHAT GOOD DID I DO THIS DAY?

_____

_____

_____

_____

_____

_____

_____

Date

· ORDER ·

"Let each part of your business have its time."

As Franklin himself did, chart out an idealized twenty-four-hour schedule for yourself for a normal day. Pay particular attention to those parts of your day that you have the most control over managing—such as your "free" time, for example.

_____

_____

_____

_____

_____

_____

_____

_____

_____

_____

_____

_____

_____

_____

_____
Date

Vicious Actions are not hurtful because they are forbidden,
but forbidden because they are hurtful.

WHAT GOOD SHALL I DO THIS DAY?	WHAT GOOD DID I DO THIS DAY?

Date

WHAT GOOD SHALL I DO THIS DAY?	WHAT GOOD DID I DO THIS DAY?

Date

WHAT GOOD SHALL I DO THIS DAY?	WHAT GOOD DID I DO THIS DAY?

Date

• RESOLUTION •

"Resolve to perform what you ought."

Is there a "duty" either to yourself or others that you have ignored or failed to perform? What is it, and how can you work toward achieving it?

_____

_____

_____

_____

_____

_____

_____

_____

_____

_____

_____

_____

_____

Date

In reality there is perhaps no one of our natural Passions
so hard to subdue as Pride.

WHAT GOOD SHALL I DO THIS DAY?	WHAT GOOD DID I DO THIS DAY?

Date

WHAT GOOD SHALL I DO THIS DAY?

_____

_____

_____

_____

_____

_____

_____

WHAT GOOD DID I DO THIS DAY?

_____

_____

_____

_____

_____

_____

_____

_____
Date

WHAT GOOD SHALL I DO THIS DAY?

_____

_____

_____

_____

_____

_____

_____

WHAT GOOD DID I DO THIS DAY?

_____

_____

_____

_____

_____

_____

_____

_____
Date

WHAT GOOD SHALL I DO THIS DAY?

_____

_____

_____

_____

_____

_____

_____

WHAT GOOD DID I DO THIS DAY?

_____

_____

_____

_____

_____

_____

_____

Date

• FRUGALITY •

"Make no expense but to do good to others or yourself.
Waste nothing."

What does frugality look like in your life? How can you curb wasteful expenditures?

_____

_____

_____

_____

_____

_____

_____

_____

_____

_____

_____

_____

_____

Date

WHAT GOOD SHALL I DO THIS DAY?	WHAT GOOD DID I DO THIS DAY?

_____
Date

WHAT GOOD SHALL I DO THIS DAY?	WHAT GOOD DID I DO THIS DAY?

_____
Date

There is certainly scarce any Part of a Man's Life in which
he appears more silly and ridiculous, than when he makes his
first Onset into Courtship.

WHAT GOOD SHALL I DO THIS DAY?	WHAT GOOD DID I DO THIS DAY?

_____

Date

WHAT GOOD SHALL I DO THIS DAY?

WHAT GOOD DID I DO THIS DAY?

Date

WHAT GOOD SHALL I DO THIS DAY?	WHAT GOOD DID I DO THIS DAY?
_____	_____
_____	_____
_____	_____
_____	_____
_____	_____

Date

WHAT GOOD SHALL I DO THIS DAY?	WHAT GOOD DID I DO THIS DAY?
_____	_____
_____	_____
_____	_____
_____	_____
_____	_____

Date

• INDUSTRY •

"Cut off all unnecessary actions."

When we think of being industrious, we often consider where we "waste" our free time rather than how we approach the actual task at hand. Is there any way you can be more efficient with your time at work?

_____

_____

_____

_____

_____

_____

_____

_____

_____

_____

_____

_____

_____

_____

_____

Date

WHAT GOOD SHALL I DO THIS DAY?

_____

_____

_____

_____

_____

_____

_____

WHAT GOOD DID I DO THIS DAY?

_____

_____

_____

_____

_____

_____

_____

_____
Date

*An inclination joined with an ability to serve mankind,
one's country, friends, and family should indeed be the great
aim and end of all learning.*

WHAT GOOD SHALL I DO THIS DAY?	WHAT GOOD DID I DO THIS DAY?

Date

WHAT GOOD SHALL I DO THIS DAY?

WHAT GOOD DID I DO THIS DAY?

Date

WHAT GOOD SHALL I DO THIS DAY?

_____

_____

_____

_____

_____

_____

_____

WHAT GOOD DID I DO THIS DAY?

_____

_____

_____

_____

_____

_____

_____

_____

Date

"Use no hurtful deceit."

For the next few days, pay special attention to the words you use. Try to do no harm in thought and deed. Check back to this space and write about your success or failure.

_____

_____

_____

_____

_____

_____

_____

_____

_____

_____

_____

_____

_____

_____

_____

_____

_____
Date

*I experienced the truth of the observation that after getting
the first £100, it is more easy to get the second.*

WHAT GOOD SHALL I DO THIS DAY?	WHAT GOOD DID I DO THIS DAY?

_____

Date

WHAT GOOD SHALL I DO THIS DAY?	WHAT GOOD DID I DO THIS DAY?

Date

WHAT GOOD SHALL I DO THIS DAY?	WHAT GOOD DID I DO THIS DAY?

Date

In what ways can you be more equitable in your daily life?

_____

_____

_____

_____

_____

_____

_____

_____

_____

_____

_____

_____

_____

_____

_____

_____

_____

Date

If we were as industrious to become Good, as to make ourselves
Great, we should become really Great by being Good.

WHAT GOOD SHALL I DO THIS DAY?	WHAT GOOD DID I DO THIS DAY?

Date

WHAT GOOD SHALL I DO THIS DAY?

_____

_____

_____

_____

_____

_____

_____

WHAT GOOD DID I DO THIS DAY?

_____

_____

_____

_____

_____

_____

_____

_____
Date

· MODERATION ·

"Avoid extremes."

What is an indulgent expense or activity in your life you'd like to curb? How would it change your life to do so?

_____

_____

_____

_____

_____

_____

_____

_____

_____

_____

_____

_____

_____

_____

_____

_____

_____
Date

How many Impertinences do we daily suffer with great Uneasiness,
because we have not the courage enough to discover our Dislike?

WHAT GOOD SHALL I DO THIS DAY?	WHAT GOOD DID I DO THIS DAY?

Date

WHAT GOOD SHALL I DO THIS DAY?

_____

_____

_____

_____

_____

_____

_____

WHAT GOOD DID I DO THIS DAY?

_____

_____

_____

_____

_____

_____

_____

_____
Date

WHAT GOOD SHALL I DO THIS DAY?

_____

_____

_____

_____

_____

_____

_____

WHAT GOOD DID I DO THIS DAY?

_____

_____

_____

_____

_____

_____

_____

_____

Date

• TRANQUILITY •

"Be not disturbed at trifles."

When are you most at peace? Why?

_____

_____

_____

_____

_____

_____

_____

_____

_____

_____

_____

_____

_____

_____

_____

_____

_____

Date

WHAT GOOD SHALL I DO THIS DAY?	WHAT GOOD DID I DO THIS DAY?

Date

WHAT GOOD SHALL I DO THIS DAY?	WHAT GOOD DID I DO THIS DAY?

Date

Men will always be powerfully influenced in their Opinions and Actions by what appears to be their particular interest.

WHAT GOOD SHALL I DO THIS DAY?	WHAT GOOD DID I DO THIS DAY?

Date

WHAT GOOD SHALL I DO THIS DAY?

_____

_____

_____

_____

_____

_____

_____

WHAT GOOD DID I DO THIS DAY?

_____

_____

_____

_____

_____

_____

_____

_____

Date

WHAT GOOD SHALL I DO THIS DAY?	WHAT GOOD DID I DO THIS DAY?

Date

WHAT GOOD SHALL I DO THIS DAY?	WHAT GOOD DID I DO THIS DAY?

Date

Today's devotional: Franklin, quoting the Bible, believed in praising that which is "true, honest, just, pure, lovely, or of good report." Write a few sentences of praise or gratitude for something good in your life or the world at large.

_____

_____

_____

_____

_____

_____

_____

_____

_____

_____

_____

_____

_____

_____

_____

_____

_____

_____

Date

WHAT GOOD SHALL I DO THIS DAY?

WHAT GOOD DID I DO THIS DAY?

Date

Endeavour to be perfect in the calling you are engaged in;
and be assiduous in every part thereof.

WHAT GOOD SHALL I DO THIS DAY?	WHAT GOOD DID I DO THIS DAY?

Date

WHAT GOOD SHALL I DO THIS DAY?

_____

_____

_____

_____

_____

_____

_____

WHAT GOOD DID I DO THIS DAY?

_____

_____

_____

_____

_____

_____

_____

_____

Date

WHAT GOOD SHALL I DO THIS DAY?

WHAT GOOD DID I DO THIS DAY?

Date

Where are you the least efficient in your daily activities? Why?

_____

_____

_____

_____

_____

_____

_____

_____

_____

_____

_____

_____

_____

_____

_____

_____

_____

_____

_____

Date

Strive to maintain a fair character in the world. That will be the best means for advancing your credit, gaining you the most flourishing trade, and enlarging your fortune.

WHAT GOOD SHALL I DO THIS DAY?	WHAT GOOD DID I DO THIS DAY?

Date

WHAT GOOD SHALL I DO THIS DAY?	WHAT GOOD DID I DO THIS DAY?

_____
Date

WHAT GOOD SHALL I DO THIS DAY?	WHAT GOOD DID I DO THIS DAY?

_____
Date

Where are you the most efficient in your daily activities? Any lessons to be learned from this success?

_____

_____

_____

_____

_____

_____

_____

_____

_____

_____

_____

_____

_____

_____

_____

_____

_____

_____
Date

Industry [is] the natural means of acquiring wealth, honour,
and reputation; as idleness is of poverty, shame, and disgrace.

WHAT GOOD SHALL I DO THIS DAY?	WHAT GOOD DID I DO THIS DAY?

Date

WHAT GOOD SHALL I DO THIS DAY?

_____

_____

_____

_____

_____

_____

_____

WHAT GOOD DID I DO THIS DAY?

_____

_____

_____

_____

_____

_____

_____

_____

Date

Do you have a major financial or career goal for your life? What is it? Think of a weekly exercise you can do to help with this goal.

_____

_____

_____

_____

_____

_____

_____

_____

_____

_____

_____

_____

_____

_____

_____

_____

_____

_____

_____

_____

Date

Never keep borrow'd Money an hour beyond the Time you promis'd,
lest a Disappointment shuts up your friend's Purse forever.

WHAT GOOD SHALL I DO THIS DAY?	WHAT GOOD DID I DO THIS DAY?

Date

WHAT GOOD SHALL I DO THIS DAY?

_____

_____

_____

_____

_____

_____

_____

WHAT GOOD DID I DO THIS DAY?

_____

_____

_____

_____

_____

_____

_____

Date

WHAT GOOD SHALL I DO THIS DAY?

_____

_____

_____

_____

_____

_____

_____

WHAT GOOD DID I DO THIS DAY?

_____

_____

_____

_____

_____

_____

_____

Date

Are there any social rifts in your life that you wish you could repair?

Date

WHAT GOOD SHALL I DO THIS DAY?	WHAT GOOD DID I DO THIS DAY?
_____	_____
_____	_____
_____	_____
_____	_____
_____	_____

Date

WHAT GOOD SHALL I DO THIS DAY?	WHAT GOOD DID I DO THIS DAY?
_____	_____
_____	_____
_____	_____
_____	_____
_____	_____

Date

The Way to Wealth, if you desire it, is as plain as the Way to Market.
It depends chiefly on two Words, INDUSTRY and FRUGALITY.

WHAT GOOD SHALL I DO THIS DAY?	WHAT GOOD DID I DO THIS DAY?

Date

WHAT GOOD SHALL I DO THIS DAY?

WHAT GOOD DID I DO THIS DAY?

Date

WHAT GOOD SHALL I DO THIS DAY?	WHAT GOOD DID I DO THIS DAY?

Date

WHAT GOOD SHALL I DO THIS DAY?	WHAT GOOD DID I DO THIS DAY?

Date

Who turns to you for advice, big or small? What are some ways you might help this person achieve their goals?

_____

_____

_____

_____

_____

_____

_____

_____

_____

_____

_____

_____

_____

_____

_____

_____

_____

_____

_____

_____

_____

Date

WHAT GOOD SHALL I DO THIS DAY?

WHAT GOOD DID I DO THIS DAY?

Date

Waste neither Time nor Money, but make the best Use of both.

WHAT GOOD SHALL I DO THIS DAY?	WHAT GOOD DID I DO THIS DAY?

Date

WHAT GOOD SHALL I DO THIS DAY?

WHAT GOOD DID I DO THIS DAY?

_____
Date

WHAT GOOD SHALL I DO THIS DAY?

WHAT GOOD DID I DO THIS DAY?

Date

183

Do you have an exercise regime? If so, is there any way you can improve it? If not, do you think you would be happier with one?

_____

_____

_____

_____

_____

_____

_____

_____

_____

_____

_____

_____

_____

_____

_____

_____

_____

_____

_____

_____
Date

*Jesters take more Freedom with Friends than they would dare
to do with others, little thinking how much deeper we are wounded
by an affront from one we love.*

WHAT GOOD SHALL I DO THIS DAY?	WHAT GOOD DID I DO THIS DAY?

Date

WHAT GOOD SHALL I DO THIS DAY?	WHAT GOOD DID I DO THIS DAY?

Date

WHAT GOOD SHALL I DO THIS DAY?	WHAT GOOD DID I DO THIS DAY?

Date

What are you anxious about today? Why?

_____

_____

_____

_____

_____

_____

_____

_____

_____

_____

_____

_____

_____

_____

_____

_____

_____

_____

_____

_____

_____

_____

Date

WHAT GOOD SHALL I DO THIS DAY?

_____

_____

_____

_____

_____

_____

_____

WHAT GOOD DID I DO THIS DAY?

_____

_____

_____

_____

_____

_____

_____

_____

Date

WHAT GOOD SHALL I DO THIS DAY?

_____

_____

_____

_____

_____

_____

_____

_____

WHAT GOOD DID I DO THIS DAY?

_____

_____

_____

_____

_____

_____

_____

_____

Date

Throw enough dirt, and some will stick.

WHAT GOOD SHALL I DO THIS DAY?	WHAT GOOD DID I DO THIS DAY?

_____

Date

WHAT GOOD SHALL I DO THIS DAY?

WHAT GOOD DID I DO THIS DAY?

Date

WHAT GOOD SHALL I DO THIS DAY?

_____

_____

_____

_____

_____

_____

_____

WHAT GOOD DID I DO THIS DAY?

_____

_____

_____

_____

_____

_____

_____

_____

Date

WHAT GOOD SHALL I DO THIS DAY?

WHAT GOOD DID I DO THIS DAY?

Date

What recent personal achievement are you the most proud of? Why?

_____

_____

_____

_____

_____

_____

_____

_____

_____

_____

_____

_____

_____

_____

_____

_____

_____

_____

_____

_____

_____

Date

WHAT GOOD SHALL I DO THIS DAY?	WHAT GOOD DID I DO THIS DAY?

Date

WHAT GOOD SHALL I DO THIS DAY?	WHAT GOOD DID I DO THIS DAY?

Date

When truth has fair play, it will always prevail over falsehood.

WHAT GOOD SHALL I DO THIS DAY?	WHAT GOOD DID I DO THIS DAY?

Date

WHAT GOOD SHALL I DO THIS DAY?

WHAT GOOD DID I DO THIS DAY?

Date

WHAT GOOD SHALL I DO THIS DAY?	WHAT GOOD DID I DO THIS DAY?

Date

WHAT GOOD SHALL I DO THIS DAY?	WHAT GOOD DID I DO THIS DAY?

Date

Are there any lessons you learned in childhood that are still relevant to you today?

_____

_____

_____

_____

_____

_____

_____

_____

_____

_____

_____

_____

_____

_____

_____

_____

_____

_____

_____
Date

WHAT GOOD SHALL I DO THIS DAY?

_____

_____

_____

_____

_____

_____

_____

WHAT GOOD DID I DO THIS DAY?

_____

_____

_____

_____

_____

_____

_____

_____

Date

*"What will the world say of me if I act thus?" is often
a reflection strong enough to enable us to resist the
most powerful temptation to vice or folly.*

WHAT GOOD SHALL I DO THIS DAY?	WHAT GOOD DID I DO THIS DAY?

Date

WHAT GOOD SHALL I DO THIS DAY?

_____

_____

_____

_____

_____

_____

_____

WHAT GOOD DID I DO THIS DAY?

_____

_____

_____

_____

_____

_____

_____

_____

Date

WHAT GOOD SHALL I DO THIS DAY?

WHAT GOOD DID I DO THIS DAY?

Date

203

Try to describe your political creed in five sentences below. Think about ways you can better merge your creed with actions in your daily life.

_____

_____

_____

_____

_____

_____

_____

_____

_____

_____

_____

_____

_____

_____

_____

_____

_____

_____

_____

_____
Date

When nature gave us tears, she gave us leave to weep.

WHAT GOOD SHALL I DO THIS DAY?	WHAT GOOD DID I DO THIS DAY?

Date

WHAT GOOD SHALL I DO THIS DAY?	WHAT GOOD DID I DO THIS DAY?
_____	_____
_____	_____
_____	_____
_____	_____
_____	_____

Date

WHAT GOOD SHALL I DO THIS DAY?	WHAT GOOD DID I DO THIS DAY?
_____	_____
_____	_____
_____	_____
_____	_____
_____	_____

Date

Have you read or heard of any news story recently that gives you hope? An advancement in science or medicine? A human-interest story?

_____

_____

_____

_____

_____

_____

_____

_____

_____

_____

_____

_____

_____

_____

_____

_____

_____

_____

_____

Date

Travelling is one way of lengthening Life, at least in Appearance.

WHAT GOOD SHALL I DO THIS DAY?	WHAT GOOD DID I DO THIS DAY?

Date

WHAT GOOD SHALL I DO THIS DAY?

_____

_____

_____

_____

_____

_____

_____

WHAT GOOD DID I DO THIS DAY?

_____

_____

_____

_____

_____

_____

_____

_____
Date

What do you like most about the place you live and the community you are part of?

_____

_____

_____

_____

_____

_____

_____

_____

_____

_____

_____

_____

_____

_____

_____

_____

_____

_____

_____
Date

Idleness and Pride tax with a heavier hand than
Kings and Parliaments.

WHAT GOOD SHALL I DO THIS DAY?	WHAT GOOD DID I DO THIS DAY?

Date

WHAT GOOD SHALL I DO THIS DAY?

_____

_____

_____

_____

_____

_____

_____

WHAT GOOD DID I DO THIS DAY?

_____

_____

_____

_____

_____

_____

_____

_____
Date

WHAT GOOD SHALL I DO THIS DAY?

_____

_____

_____

_____

_____

_____

_____

WHAT GOOD DID I DO THIS DAY?

_____

_____

_____

_____

_____

_____

_____

_____
Date

What is something you'd like to change in your workplace or community? Are there any realistic ways to attempt to do so?

_____

_____

_____

_____

_____

_____

_____

_____

_____

_____

_____

_____

_____

_____

_____

_____

_____

_____

_____

_____
Date

WHAT GOOD SHALL I DO THIS DAY?	WHAT GOOD DID I DO THIS DAY?

_____
Date

WHAT GOOD SHALL I DO THIS DAY?	WHAT GOOD DID I DO THIS DAY?

_____
Date

'Tis Convenient to have at least one Enemy, who by his Readiness to revile one on all Occasions, may make one careful of one's conduct.

WHAT GOOD SHALL I DO THIS DAY?	WHAT GOOD DID I DO THIS DAY?

Date

WHAT GOOD SHALL I DO THIS DAY?

\
\
\
\
\
\
\

WHAT GOOD DID I DO THIS DAY?

\
\
\
\
\
\
\

\
Date

WHAT GOOD SHALL I DO THIS DAY?	WHAT GOOD DID I DO THIS DAY?

_____
Date

WHAT GOOD SHALL I DO THIS DAY?	WHAT GOOD DID I DO THIS DAY?

_____
Date

Can you think of a leader in your workplace or community that you admire? What qualities does she exhibit that you would like to grow in your own life?

_____

Date

WHAT GOOD SHALL I DO THIS DAY?

_____

_____

_____

_____

_____

_____

_____

WHAT GOOD DID I DO THIS DAY?

_____

_____

_____

_____

_____

_____

_____

_____

Date

Many People lead bad lives that would gladly lead good ones,
but know not how to make the Change.

WHAT GOOD SHALL I DO THIS DAY?	WHAT GOOD DID I DO THIS DAY?

Date

WHAT GOOD SHALL I DO THIS DAY?

_____

_____

_____

_____

_____

_____

_____

WHAT GOOD DID I DO THIS DAY?

_____

_____

_____

_____

_____

_____

_____

_____

Date

WHAT GOOD SHALL I DO THIS DAY?

WHAT GOOD DID I DO THIS DAY?

Date

What's a common complaint you've heard about your behavior or work? Do you believe it? Can you improve on it?

_____

_____

_____

_____

_____

_____

_____

_____

_____

_____

_____

_____

_____

_____

_____

_____

_____

Date

Constancy is a virtue never too highly prized, and whose true worth is by few rightly understood.

WHAT GOOD SHALL I DO THIS DAY?	WHAT GOOD DID I DO THIS DAY?

Date

WHAT GOOD SHALL I DO THIS DAY?	WHAT GOOD DID I DO THIS DAY?

_____

Date

WHAT GOOD SHALL I DO THIS DAY?	WHAT GOOD DID I DO THIS DAY?

_____

Date

Today's devotional: Franklin, quoting the Bible, believed in praising that which is "true, honest, just, pure, lovely, or of good report." Write a few sentences of praise or gratitude for something good in your life or the world at large.

_____

_____

_____

_____

_____

_____

_____

_____

_____

_____

_____

_____

_____

_____

_____

_____

_____

Date

A Man who has no End in View, no Design to pursue,
is like an irresolute Master of a Ship at Sea, that can fix
upon no one Port to steer her to, and consequently can
call not one wind favourable to his wishes.

WHAT GOOD SHALL I DO THIS DAY?	WHAT GOOD DID I DO THIS DAY?

Date

WHAT GOOD SHALL I DO THIS DAY?

WHAT GOOD DID I DO THIS DAY?

_____

Date

What place does religious or spiritual thought have in your life? Do you wish it could be more prevalent? More helpful?

_____

_____

_____

_____

_____

_____

_____

_____

_____

_____

_____

_____

_____

_____

_____

_____

Date

Without steadiness or perseverance no virtue can long subsist.

WHAT GOOD SHALL I DO THIS DAY?	WHAT GOOD DID I DO THIS DAY?

Date

WHAT GOOD SHALL I DO THIS DAY?

WHAT GOOD DID I DO THIS DAY?

Date

WHAT GOOD SHALL I DO THIS DAY?

WHAT GOOD DID I DO THIS DAY?

Date

233

Is there any task in your work or community that you have been avoiding doing?

_____

_____

_____

_____

_____

_____

_____

_____

_____

_____

_____

_____

_____

_____

_____

_____

_____

_____

_____

_____

Date

WHAT GOOD SHALL I DO THIS DAY?	WHAT GOOD DID I DO THIS DAY?

Date

WHAT GOOD SHALL I DO THIS DAY?	WHAT GOOD DID I DO THIS DAY?

Date

Does it not require as much pains, study, and application to become truly wise and strictly good as to become rich?

WHAT GOOD SHALL I DO THIS DAY?	WHAT GOOD DID I DO THIS DAY?

Date

WHAT GOOD SHALL I DO THIS DAY?

_____

_____

_____

_____

_____

_____

_____

WHAT GOOD DID I DO THIS DAY?

_____

_____

_____

_____

_____

_____

_____

_____

Date

WHAT GOOD SHALL I DO THIS DAY?	WHAT GOOD DID I DO THIS DAY?

Date

WHAT GOOD SHALL I DO THIS DAY?	WHAT GOOD DID I DO THIS DAY?

Date

In his notes on virtue, Franklin freely admitted to being challenged by his own sense of pride and by his tendency to be disorganized. What "fault" would you freely admit to? Are there ways to lessen its impact in your life?

_____

_____

_____

_____

_____

_____

_____

_____

_____

_____

_____

_____

_____

_____

_____

_____

_____
Date

WHAT GOOD SHALL I DO THIS DAY?

_____

_____

_____

_____

_____

_____

_____

WHAT GOOD DID I DO THIS DAY?

_____

_____

_____

_____

_____

_____

_____

_____

Date

Which is the best to make a Friend of, a wise and good man that is poor or a rich man that is neither wise nor good?

WHAT GOOD SHALL I DO THIS DAY?	WHAT GOOD DID I DO THIS DAY?

Date

WHAT GOOD SHALL I DO THIS DAY?

WHAT GOOD DID I DO THIS DAY?

Date

WHAT GOOD SHALL I DO THIS DAY?

_____

_____

_____

_____

_____

_____

_____

WHAT GOOD DID I DO THIS DAY?

_____

_____

_____

_____

_____

_____

_____

_____

Date

In what avenue of your life are you excelling? If you were to describe your success to someone, what wisdom might they gain from it?

_____

_____

_____

_____

_____

_____

_____

_____

_____

_____

_____

_____

_____

_____

_____

_____

_____

_____

_____

Date

No man is truly wise but who hath been deceived.

WHAT GOOD SHALL I DO THIS DAY?	WHAT GOOD DID I DO THIS DAY?

Date

WHAT GOOD SHALL I DO THIS DAY?	WHAT GOOD DID I DO THIS DAY?

Date

WHAT GOOD SHALL I DO THIS DAY?	WHAT GOOD DID I DO THIS DAY?

Date

Try to spend today putting the needs of others before your own as often and as honestly as you can. Write about your experience here.

_____

_____

_____

_____

_____

_____

_____

_____

_____

_____

_____

_____

_____

_____

_____

_____

_____

_____

_____

_____

Date

Men are naturally benevolent as well as selfish. For whence can arise the pleasure you feel after having done a good-natured thing, if not hence that you had before strong humane and kind inclinations in your nature?

WHAT GOOD SHALL I DO THIS DAY?	WHAT GOOD DID I DO THIS DAY?

Date

WHAT GOOD SHALL I DO THIS DAY?

_____

_____

_____

_____

_____

_____

_____

WHAT GOOD DID I DO THIS DAY?

_____

_____

_____

_____

_____

_____

_____

_____

Date

WHAT GOOD SHALL I DO THIS DAY?

WHAT GOOD DID I DO THIS DAY?

Date

WHAT GOOD SHALL I DO THIS DAY?

_____

_____

_____

_____

_____

_____

_____

WHAT GOOD DID I DO THIS DAY?

_____

_____

_____

_____

_____

_____

_____

_____

Date

When was the last time you were the recipient of an unexpected act of kindness?

_____

_____

_____

_____

_____

_____

_____

_____

_____

_____

_____

_____

_____

_____

_____

_____

_____

_____

_____

Date

WHAT GOOD SHALL I DO THIS DAY?	WHAT GOOD DID I DO THIS DAY?

Date

WHAT GOOD SHALL I DO THIS DAY?	WHAT GOOD DID I DO THIS DAY?

Date

I began the world with this maxim:
that no trade can subsist without returns.

WHAT GOOD SHALL I DO THIS DAY?	WHAT GOOD DID I DO THIS DAY?

Date

WHAT GOOD SHALL I DO THIS DAY?

WHAT GOOD DID I DO THIS DAY?

Date

255

WHAT GOOD SHALL I DO THIS DAY?	WHAT GOOD DID I DO THIS DAY?

Date

WHAT GOOD SHALL I DO THIS DAY?	WHAT GOOD DID I DO THIS DAY?

Date

In *Poor Richard's Almanack*, Franklin wrote, "The way to be safe, is never to be secure." What does this mean to you and your life? Is it true or false?

_____

_____

_____

_____

_____

_____

_____

_____

_____

_____

_____

_____

_____

_____

_____

_____

_____

Date

WHAT GOOD SHALL I DO THIS DAY?

_____

_____

_____

_____

_____

_____

_____

WHAT GOOD DID I DO THIS DAY?

_____

_____

_____

_____

_____

_____

_____

_____

Date

There is hardly such a thing as a friend sincere or rash
enough to acquaint us freely with our faults.

WHAT GOOD SHALL I DO THIS DAY?	WHAT GOOD DID I DO THIS DAY?

Date

WHAT GOOD SHALL I DO THIS DAY?

_____

_____

_____

_____

_____

_____

_____

WHAT GOOD DID I DO THIS DAY?

_____

_____

_____

_____

_____

_____

_____

_____
Date

WHAT GOOD SHALL I DO THIS DAY?

_____

_____

_____

_____

_____

_____

_____

WHAT GOOD DID I DO THIS DAY?

_____

_____

_____

_____

_____

_____

_____

_____

Date

Who is the most charitable person you know? What makes them thus?

_____

_____

_____

_____

_____

_____

_____

_____

_____

_____

_____

_____

_____

_____

_____

_____

_____

_____

_____

_____

_____

Date

Reading makes a full man, meditation a profound man,
discourse a clear man.

WHAT GOOD SHALL I DO THIS DAY?	WHAT GOOD DID I DO THIS DAY?

Date

WHAT GOOD SHALL I DO THIS DAY?	WHAT GOOD DID I DO THIS DAY?
_____	_____
_____	_____
_____	_____
_____	_____
_____	_____

Date

WHAT GOOD SHALL I DO THIS DAY?	WHAT GOOD DID I DO THIS DAY?
_____	_____
_____	_____
_____	_____
_____	_____
_____	_____

Date

Write about a misfortune you have suffered recently.

_____

_____

_____

_____

_____

_____

_____

_____

_____

_____

_____

_____

_____

_____

_____

_____

_____

_____

_____

_____

_____

Date

Anger and folly walk cheek by jowl;
repentance treads on both their heels.

WHAT GOOD SHALL I DO THIS DAY?	WHAT GOOD DID I DO THIS DAY?

_____

Date

WHAT GOOD SHALL I DO THIS DAY?

WHAT GOOD DID I DO THIS DAY?

Date

267

What does family mean to you? Where are the bonds of your family strongest?

_____

_____

_____

_____

_____

_____

_____

_____

_____

_____

_____

_____

_____

_____

_____

_____

_____

_____

_____

Date

How few there are who have courage enough to own
their faults, or resolution enough to mend them.

WHAT GOOD SHALL I DO THIS DAY?	WHAT GOOD DID I DO THIS DAY?

Date

WHAT GOOD SHALL I DO THIS DAY?

_____

_____

_____

_____

_____

_____

_____

WHAT GOOD DID I DO THIS DAY?

_____

_____

_____

_____

_____

_____

_____

_____

Date

WHAT GOOD SHALL I DO THIS DAY?

_____

_____

_____

_____

_____

_____

_____

WHAT GOOD DID I DO THIS DAY?

_____

_____

_____

_____

_____

_____

_____

_____

Date

What are you curious about outside your own area of expertise?

_____

_____

_____

_____

_____

_____

_____

_____

_____

_____

_____

_____

_____

_____

_____

_____

_____

_____

_____

_____
Date

WHAT GOOD SHALL I DO THIS DAY?	WHAT GOOD DID I DO THIS DAY?

Date

WHAT GOOD SHALL I DO THIS DAY?	WHAT GOOD DID I DO THIS DAY?

Date

Experience keeps a dear school, yet fools would learn in no other.

WHAT GOOD SHALL I DO THIS DAY?	WHAT GOOD DID I DO THIS DAY?

Date

WHAT GOOD SHALL I DO THIS DAY?

WHAT GOOD DID I DO THIS DAY?

Date

WHAT GOOD SHALL I DO THIS DAY?	WHAT GOOD DID I DO THIS DAY?

Date

WHAT GOOD SHALL I DO THIS DAY?	WHAT GOOD DID I DO THIS DAY?

Date

Are you better at giving direction or taking direction?

_____

_____

_____

_____

_____

_____

_____

_____

_____

_____

_____

_____

_____

_____

_____

_____

_____

_____

_____
Date

WHAT GOOD SHALL I DO THIS DAY?

_____

_____

_____

_____

_____

_____

_____

WHAT GOOD DID I DO THIS DAY?

_____

_____

_____

_____

_____

_____

_____

_____

Date

If you'd lose a troublesome visitor, lend him money.

WHAT GOOD SHALL I DO THIS DAY?	WHAT GOOD DID I DO THIS DAY?

Date

WHAT GOOD SHALL I DO THIS DAY?

_____

_____

_____

_____

_____

_____

_____

WHAT GOOD DID I DO THIS DAY?

_____

_____

_____

_____

_____

_____

_____

_____
Date

WHAT GOOD SHALL I DO THIS DAY?

WHAT GOOD DID I DO THIS DAY?

Date

Today's devotional: Franklin, quoting the Bible, believed in praising that which is "true, honest, just, pure, lovely, or of good report." Write a few sentences of praise or gratitude for something good in your life or the world at large.

_____

_____

_____

_____

_____

_____

_____

_____

_____

_____

_____

_____

_____

_____

_____

_____

_____

_____

_____

Date

'Tis easier to prevent bad habits then to break them.

WHAT GOOD SHALL I DO THIS DAY?	WHAT GOOD DID I DO THIS DAY?

Date

WHAT GOOD SHALL I DO THIS DAY?	WHAT GOOD DID I DO THIS DAY?

_____

Date

WHAT GOOD SHALL I DO THIS DAY?	WHAT GOOD DID I DO THIS DAY?

_____

Date

If someone asked you what is the key to a happy life, what would you tell them?

_____

_____

_____

_____

_____

_____

_____

_____

_____

_____

_____

_____

_____

_____

_____

_____

_____

_____

_____

_____

Date

He that resolves to mend hereafter resolves not to mend now.

WHAT GOOD SHALL I DO THIS DAY?	WHAT GOOD DID I DO THIS DAY?

Date

WHAT GOOD SHALL I DO THIS DAY?

_____

_____

_____

_____

_____

_____

_____

WHAT GOOD DID I DO THIS DAY?

_____

_____

_____

_____

_____

_____

_____

_____

Date

In *Poor Richard's Almanack*, Franklin wrote, "Be always ashamed to catch yourself idle." Is this maxim true for you?

_____

_____

_____

_____

_____

_____

_____

_____

_____

_____

_____

_____

_____

_____

_____

_____

_____

_____

_____

_____

Date

Strive to be the greatest man in your country, and you may
be disappointed; strive to be the best, and you may succeed.
He may well win the race that runs himself.

WHAT GOOD SHALL I DO THIS DAY?	WHAT GOOD DID I DO THIS DAY?

Date

WHAT GOOD SHALL I DO THIS DAY?

WHAT GOOD DID I DO THIS DAY?

Date

WHAT GOOD SHALL I DO THIS DAY?

_____

_____

_____

_____

_____

_____

_____

_____

WHAT GOOD DID I DO THIS DAY?

_____

_____

_____

_____

_____

_____

_____

_____

_____

Date

What do you see as the biggest challenge facing your work or community in the coming weeks? In the next year? In the next five years?

_____

_____

_____

_____

_____

_____

_____

_____

_____

_____

_____

_____

_____

_____

_____

_____

_____

_____

_____

Date

WHAT GOOD SHALL I DO THIS DAY?	WHAT GOOD DID I DO THIS DAY?
_____	_____
_____	_____
_____	_____
_____	_____
_____	_____

_____

Date

WHAT GOOD SHALL I DO THIS DAY?	WHAT GOOD DID I DO THIS DAY?
_____	_____
_____	_____
_____	_____
_____	_____
_____	_____

_____

Date

He that cannot bear other people's passions cannot govern his own.

WHAT GOOD SHALL I DO THIS DAY?	WHAT GOOD DID I DO THIS DAY?

Date

WHAT GOOD SHALL I DO THIS DAY?

_____

_____

_____

_____

_____

_____

_____

WHAT GOOD DID I DO THIS DAY?

_____

_____

_____

_____

_____

_____

_____

_____
Date

WHAT GOOD SHALL I DO THIS DAY?	WHAT GOOD DID I DO THIS DAY?

Date

WHAT GOOD SHALL I DO THIS DAY?	WHAT GOOD DID I DO THIS DAY?

Date

What improvements would you like to see in your neighborhood or community? Who would benefit from these improvements?

_____

_____

_____

_____

_____

_____

_____

_____

_____

_____

_____

_____

_____

_____

_____

_____

_____

_____

_____

_____

Date

WHAT GOOD SHALL I DO THIS DAY?

_____

_____

_____

_____

_____

_____

_____

WHAT GOOD DID I DO THIS DAY?

_____

_____

_____

_____

_____

_____

_____

_____

Date

Suspicion may be no fault, but showing it may be a great one.

WHAT GOOD SHALL I DO THIS DAY?	WHAT GOOD DID I DO THIS DAY?

Date

WHAT GOOD SHALL I DO THIS DAY?

WHAT GOOD DID I DO THIS DAY?

Date

WHAT GOOD SHALL I DO THIS DAY?

WHAT GOOD DID I DO THIS DAY?

Date

Consider your daily economy. Write down every purchase and expense you make today. Which of these was necessary, and which could you do without?

_____

_____

_____

_____

_____

_____

_____

_____

_____

_____

_____

_____

_____

_____

_____

_____

_____

_____

Date

How happy is he who can satisfy his hunger with any food,
quench his thirst with any drink, please his ear with any music?
Your man of taste is nothing but a man of distaste.

WHAT GOOD SHALL I DO THIS DAY?	WHAT GOOD DID I DO THIS DAY?

Date

WHAT GOOD SHALL I DO THIS DAY?	WHAT GOOD DID I DO THIS DAY?

Date

WHAT GOOD SHALL I DO THIS DAY?	WHAT GOOD DID I DO THIS DAY?

Date

When in a contentious discussion, Franklin wrote that he found it best to be a "humble enquirer" rather than one who "provokes contradiction." When have you encountered a situation where patience and questions served you better than argument?

_____

_____

_____

_____

_____

_____

_____

_____

_____

_____

_____

_____

_____

_____

_____

_____

_____

_____

_____

_____

Date

WHAT GOOD SHALL I DO THIS DAY?

_____

_____

_____

_____

_____

_____

_____

WHAT GOOD DID I DO THIS DAY?

_____

_____

_____

_____

_____

_____

_____

_____
Date

WHAT GOOD SHALL I DO THIS DAY?

WHAT GOOD DID I DO THIS DAY?

_____

Date

Wise men learn by others' harms; fools by their own.

WHAT GOOD SHALL I DO THIS DAY?	WHAT GOOD DID I DO THIS DAY?

Date

WHAT GOOD SHALL I DO THIS DAY?

_____

_____

_____

_____

_____

_____

_____

_____

WHAT GOOD DID I DO THIS DAY?

_____

_____

_____

_____

_____

_____

_____

_____

Date

WHAT GOOD SHALL I DO THIS DAY?

_____

_____

_____

_____

_____

_____

_____

WHAT GOOD DID I DO THIS DAY?

_____

_____

_____

_____

_____

_____

_____

_____
Date

WHAT GOOD SHALL I DO THIS DAY?

_____

_____

_____

_____

_____

_____

WHAT GOOD DID I DO THIS DAY?

_____

_____

_____

_____

_____

_____

_____

_____

Date

In *Poor Richard's Almanack*, Franklin wrote, "three good meals a day is bad living." Where in your life would a little austerity be useful?

_____

_____

_____

_____

_____

_____

_____

_____

_____

_____

_____

_____

_____

_____

_____

_____

_____

_____

_____

Date

WHAT GOOD SHALL I DO THIS DAY?	WHAT GOOD DID I DO THIS DAY?

Date

WHAT GOOD SHALL I DO THIS DAY?	WHAT GOOD DID I DO THIS DAY?

Date

Learning whether speculative or practical is the
natural source of wealth and honor.

WHAT GOOD SHALL I DO THIS DAY?	WHAT GOOD DID I DO THIS DAY?

Date

WHAT GOOD SHALL I DO THIS DAY?

WHAT GOOD DID I DO THIS DAY?

Date

WHAT GOOD SHALL I DO THIS DAY?	WHAT GOOD DID I DO THIS DAY?

_____
Date

WHAT GOOD SHALL I DO THIS DAY?	WHAT GOOD DID I DO THIS DAY?

_____
Date

What is a continuing point of contention in either your work or home life? Below, chart out the reasoning of the other side of the argument than the side you are on.

_____

_____

_____

_____

_____

_____

_____

_____

_____

_____

_____

_____

_____

_____

_____

_____

_____

_____

_____
Date

WHAT GOOD SHALL I DO THIS DAY?

_____

_____

_____

_____

_____

_____

_____

WHAT GOOD DID I DO THIS DAY?

_____

_____

_____

_____

_____

_____

_____

_____
Date

Pride is as loud a beggar as want, and a great deal more saucy.

WHAT GOOD SHALL I DO THIS DAY?	WHAT GOOD DID I DO THIS DAY?

Date

WHAT GOOD SHALL I DO THIS DAY?

_____

_____

_____

_____

_____

_____

_____

WHAT GOOD DID I DO THIS DAY?

_____

_____

_____

_____

_____

_____

_____

_____
Date

WHAT GOOD SHALL I DO THIS DAY?

_____

_____

_____

_____

_____

_____

_____

WHAT GOOD DID I DO THIS DAY?

_____

_____

_____

_____

_____

_____

_____

Date

Franklin wrote, "I think no pleasure innocent that is to Man hurtful." Does this statement seem true or false to you?

_____

_____

_____

_____

_____

_____

_____

_____

_____

_____

_____

_____

_____

_____

_____

_____

_____

_____

_____

_____
Date

'Tis hard (but glorious) to be poor and honest: an empty sack can hardly stand upright, but if it does, 'tis a stout one.

WHAT GOOD SHALL I DO THIS DAY?	WHAT GOOD DID I DO THIS DAY?

Date

WHAT GOOD SHALL I DO THIS DAY?	WHAT GOOD DID I DO THIS DAY?

_____

Date

WHAT GOOD SHALL I DO THIS DAY?	WHAT GOOD DID I DO THIS DAY?

_____

Date

In what part of your daily activities could you exhibit more compassion for others?

_____

_____

_____

_____

_____

_____

_____

_____

_____

_____

_____

_____

_____

_____

_____

_____

_____

_____

_____

Date

Love and tooth-ache have many cures, but none infallible,
except possession and dispossession.

WHAT GOOD SHALL I DO THIS DAY?	WHAT GOOD DID I DO THIS DAY?

Date

WHAT GOOD SHALL I DO THIS DAY?

_____

_____

_____

_____

_____

_____

_____

WHAT GOOD DID I DO THIS DAY?

_____

_____

_____

_____

_____

_____

_____

_____
Date

List three role models for your life. Why do you admire these people?

_____

_____

_____

_____

_____

_____

_____

_____

_____

_____

_____

_____

_____

_____

_____

_____

_____

_____

_____
Date

Today is yesterday's pupil.

WHAT GOOD SHALL I DO THIS DAY?	WHAT GOOD DID I DO THIS DAY?

Date

WHAT GOOD SHALL I DO THIS DAY?

WHAT GOOD DID I DO THIS DAY?

Date

NOTES

NOTES

NOTES

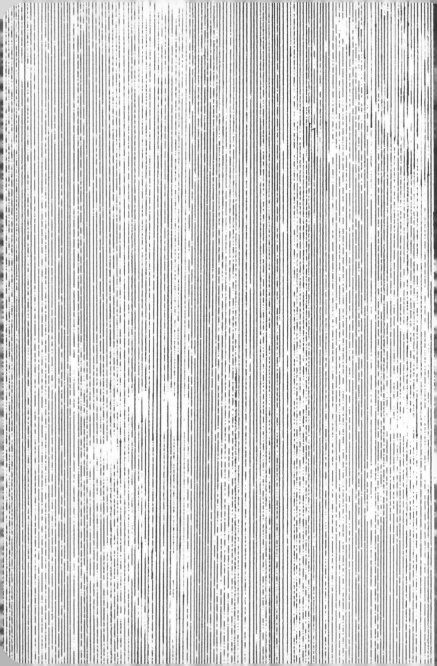

BENJAMIN FRANKLIN'S THIRTEEN VIRTUES

N°. 1

• TEMPERANCE •

Eat not to dullness. Drink not to elevation.

N°. 2

• SILENCE •

Speak not but what may benefit others or yourself.
Avoid trifling conversation.

N°. 3

• ORDER •

Let all your things have their places. Let each part of your business
have its time.

N°. 4

• RESOLUTION •

Resolve to perform what you ought. Perform without
fail what you resolve.

N°. 5

• FRUGALITY •

Make no expense but to do good to others or yourself:
i.e., Waste nothing.

N°. 6

• INDUSTRY •

Lose no time. Be always employed in something useful.
Cut off all unnecessary actions.

N°. 7

• SINCERITY •

Use no hurtful deceit. Think innocently and justly;
and if you speak, speak accordingly.

N°. 8

• JUSTICE •

Wrong none by doing injuries, or omitting the benefits
that are your duty.

N°. 9

• MODERATION •

Avoid extremes. Forbear resenting injuries so much
as you think they deserve.

N°. 10

• CLEANLINESS •

Tolerate no uncleanness in body, clothes, or habitation.

N°. 11

• TRANQUILITY •

Be not disturbed at trifles, or at accidents
common or unavoidable.

No. 12

· CHASTITY ·

Rarely use venery but for health or offspring;
never to dullness, weakness, or the injury of your
own or another's peace or reputation.

No. 13

· HUMILITY ·

Imitate Jesus and Socrates.

THE JUNTO

In 1727, a twenty-one-year-old Benjamin Franklin formed a social club of "leather apron men," that is, tradesmen, businessmen, and craftsmen. They met weekly to discuss issues of community, civil service, and how to be of mutual service to one another. Before the start of each meeting, Franklin urged each member to scan a list of twenty-four questions to direct their conversations.

1. Have you met with any thing in the author you last read, remarkable, or suitable to be communicated to the Junto? particularly in history, morality, poetry, physics, travels, mechanic arts, or other parts of knowledge?

2. What new story have you lately heard agreeable for telling in conversation?

3. Hath any citizen in your knowledge failed in his business lately, and what have you heard of the cause?

4. Have you lately heard of any citizen's thriving well, and by what means?

5. Have you lately heard how any present rich man, here or elsewhere, got his estate?

6. Do you know of any fellow citizen, who has lately done a worthy action, deserving praise and imitation? or who has committed an error proper for us to be warned against and avoid?

7. What unhappy effects of intemperance have you lately observed or heard? of imprudence? of passion? or of any other vice or folly?

8. What happy effects of temperance? of prudence? of moderation? or of any other virtue?

9. Have you or any of your acquaintance been lately sick or wounded? If so, what remedies were used, and what were their effects?

10. Who do you know that are shortly going [on] voyages or journies, if one should have occasion to send by them?

11. Do you think of any thing at present, in which the Junto may be serviceable to mankind? to their country, to their friends, or to themselves?

12. Hath any deserving stranger arrived in town since last meeting, that you heard of? and what have you heard or observed of his character or merits? and whether think you, it lies in the power of the Junto to oblige him, or encourage him as he deserves?

13. Do you know of any deserving young beginner lately set up, whom it lies in the power of the Junto any way to encourage?

14. Have you lately observed any defect in the laws of your country, of which it would be proper to move the legislature an amendment? Or do you know of any beneficial law that is wanting?

15. Have you lately observed any encroachment on the just liberties of the people?

16. Hath any body attacked your reputation lately? and what can the Junto do towards securing it?

17. Is there any man whose friendship you want, and which the Junto, or any of them, can procure for you?

18. Have you lately heard any member's character attacked, and how have you defended it?

19. Hath any man injured you, from whom it is in the power of the Junto to procure redress?

20. In what manner can the Junto, or any of them, assist you in any of your honourable designs?

21. Have you any weighty affair in hand, in which you think the advice of the Junto may be of service?

22. What benefits have you lately received from any man not present?

23. Is there any difficulty in matters of opinion, of justice, and injustice, which you would gladly have discussed at this time?

24. Do you see any thing amiss in the present customs or proceedings of the Junto, which might be amended?